CRYPTO

SECRETS FOR

BEGINNERS 2022

How To Make More Money During A Cryptocurrency Market Crash And Prepare Yourself For The Next

Gerald Hinkle

Copyright © 2021 Gerald Hinkle

All rights reserved.

DISCLAIMER

The information in this guide is for educational purposes only and should never be taken by the reader as personal financial advice.

The author will not be held liable for any financial losses incurred due to using the information in this guide.

Before making any financial investments, the reader is advised to get professional financial advice from only licensed financial advisors.

All the trademarks mentioned in this guide are properties of their respective owners, and all rights belong to them.

CONTENTS

Disclaimer	i
Introduction	1
Chapter One: Why they keep happening?	3
Chapter Two: How do I prepare?	10
Chapter Three: Doubling your money	15
Summary	32

INTRODUCTION

A bitcoin or stock market crash may be pretty frightening for many people. Nobody wants to lose any of their investment gains in the months, days, or weeks leading up to a significant drop.

Rather than hiding our heads in the sand or assuming that simply discussing crashes is fear-mongering or encouraging FUD (fear, uncertainty, doubt), the truth is that crashes are an unavoidable part of investing.

Day and night, as well as summer and winter, will always exist, and booms and busts will continue to occur too.

Another huge crash is just a matter of time, which is why it is vital that we speak about it on a regular basis, be ready, and be as prepared as possible for such events.

So, in this guide, we'll look at why crashes happen and why they continue to happen, as well as two potential crash events on the horizon right now and what we can do to lower our risk and prepare for a crash. Finally, we'll look at the top five ways to double your money in the case of a bitcoin crash.

Let's get this party started right now.

CHAPTER ONE

Why they keep happening

Have you ever thought about why crashes keep happening in the first place? We should always attempt to learn as much as possible about crashes since they are crucial in investing. This also includes the psychology behind them. Ready?

We have crashes and will continue to have more in the future for two main reasons. Here are the reasons:

1. Humans are emotional creatures

At the core of it all is the reality that we are emotional creatures who reason, rather than the other way around.

The limbic system is the brain's oldest and most powerful component, controlling our fight, flight, or freeze reaction.

It is interesting to note that this is part of the subconscious mind. So, we do not have total control over the limbic system.

Unfortunately, in times of fear, uncertainty, or anxiety, this unconscious section of the brain is awakened, causing people to panic and sell because they don't want to lose any of their financial gains.

Now – next time you wonder why people panic and sell their crypto holdings, sometimes, at up to 50% loss, remember that they are not acting on their own accord.

Rather, it is their limbic system that is acting on their behalf. And as long as the limbic system continues to be a part of us as humans, it will continue to prompt us to take knee-jerk reactions.

2. Everything in life follows a predictable pattern

The second point to consider is that things happen in cycles like with most things in life. The truth is that we have no idea how much the asset (bitcoin) is worth, which is something that everyone is trying to figure out.

Instead, what we have is what seems to be a rising and falling wave. The wave seems to be almost straight at times, rising and dipping below the straight line.

Because we don't know their genuine value, crypto assets are always overpriced, undervalued, and then overvalued.

Everyone rushes in when things are going up, raising the price far higher than it is worth. Fear and panic set in, and many start panic-selling in order to avoid losing their earnings. This pushes the value below its true worth, and the cycle continues.

This cycle continues to repeat indefinitely. First, everyone rushes in, prices start rise. More people rush in and the prices skyrocket.

People panic and start selling to take profit, and prices will begin to fall. After sometime, prices will fall below normal lines.

Next, more people will begin buying again, pushing prices up and the cycle continues to repeat.

So, as you can see – our brains and nature are unlikely to change anytime soon. This means that we will continue to have booms and busts as well as black swan events.

We've now seen the two most common causes of crypto crashes, which will continue to happen in the future.

Next, let's talk about the two possible crash occurrences that we may face in the near future.

Possible crash events

Here are two possible future events that may trigger crashes in the nearest future.

1. Regulations on the horizon

The first element that might lead to a crash is regulation, since 90 percent of cryptos pass the SEC's security test, suggesting that they should be appropriately regulated.

There's also the looming problematic infrastructure bill, which contains an ambiguous phrase about crypto brokers that, if enacted, could throw a massive monkey wrench into the works and bring the whole market down.

A stock market crisis is the second trigger on the horizon. Several of these regulatory bombs might go off at any time, bringing the market down.

2. A stock market crash

The buffet indicator, which divides equities by GDP, is flashing danger alerts right now because stock market valuations are at historically high levels.

We also have all of the unknowns, such as what happened with Covid or China's closure of bitcoin miners or, more recently, Evergrande's insolvency, which is already hurting global markets (at the time of writing).

The idea is that a catastrophic financial meltdown between now and mid 2022 isn't something we can just ignore. We must always be ready to the best of our ability.

CHAPTER TWO

How Do I Prepare?

Keeping your crypto allocation under control is the easiest thing you can do to help limit your risk.

It's important to remember that bitcoin is a high-risk asset. Yes, risk is not the same as volatility, but since the asset is also volatile, it raises your chances of panicking and selling at the wrong time.

Don't overextend yourself, depending on your position. Only invest money you can afford to lose, and the amount differs from person to person since we want to make sure we're not gambling.

Another way I decrease my risk is to structure my work into three distinct phases: accumulation, hoarding, and selling.

So, in my opinion, when the market falls by more than 50%, we enter a good period for accumulation, and you'll see that this is also when the bulk of people panic and sell.

Following that, we enter phase two, which is the time of hodling, which lasts until the market recovers and begins to make new highs, after which you determine when to take profits if the market continues to make new highs. Alternatively, you may just be hodling, depending on your aims.

Finally, you may reduce your risk by investing primarily in large-cap assets like Bitcoin and Ethereum, the Apple and Microsoft of the cryptocurrency world.

Coins and tokens that don't fall into the top 20 category are like the small caps, microcaps, and penny stocks and you should be careful with them because they pose a greater risk.

It's important to note that this isn't investment advice; rather, it's how I manage my risk and deal with the volatility of the crypto market.

Bottom-line

Crashing is a part of the investing process that cannot be avoided. It makes no difference whether we like it or not. Rather than hiding our heads in the sand, we should accept it, speak about it often, and look for ways to prepare for and even profit from crashes.

Crashes often present the best investment opportunities you'll ever have, which is why I'll keep writing about them on a regular basis.

Nobody knows what will set off the next great financial crisis; it may be legislation, a stock market meltdown, or a black swan event.

Make sure you don't overdo it with your cryptocurrency allocation. Purchase after a market dip and sell when the market achieves new highs to reduce your risk. And selling on the spur of the moment is perhaps the worst decision you can make.

Having said that, I continue to believe that crypto's long-term trend is much higher. Simply put, we'll have to deal with a lot of volatility in the short future as we go from fear to greed to green to fear.

In this section, we looked at ways to prepare for crypto crashes. In the next and last section, we'll look at strategies to double your money amid a crypto crash.

CHAPTER THREE

Doubling your money

Here are the top 5 ways to profit or quadruple your money without wasting time during a crypto crash.

#1: Purchase the dip

This may seem self-evident, but it should be since that is what every sane investor should be doing.

This is one tactic that is much more difficult to implement than it seems. And you have to be cautious not to purchase the third mid-flush just for the coin to continue to fall in value.

As tough as it may be to purchase something you've been watching the price drop, it's always the greatest moment to do so if you've done your homework beforehand.

"Be greedy when others are scared, and fearful when others are greedy," is a saying I'm sure you've heard.

"Have an open mind when others are closed minded," I'd like to add to the preceding quotation. This is because having a healthy level of fear is occasionally appropriate, but having an open mind is beneficial most of the time.

So, if China announces for the 200th time that they are going to ban crypto and everyone is afraid, and you see a nice little daily correction, it is better to be open-minded and say, "Hey, China has stated this 10099 times, and it didn't really matter in the end."

Furthermore, it's always amusing that no matter how great of a drop we observe, many people tend to forget how much money can be made by purchasing the correct dip in crypto.

A ten percent annual return is considered excellent over time in the stock market, and we are constantly offered chances to purchase crypto drops of ten, fifteen, or twenty percent. And, in many cases, it returns the same day or within a day or two after the correction, and you've made a 10 to

20% profit in a day or two. That's an S&P 500 return in a matter of days.

Many individuals will remark that they purchased the dip and it continued dropping, or that they waited to buy the dip because they anticipated it would go lower, and now it has returned to an all-time high, and they lost out on all of the money they might have gained.

Here's the thing: if you're trying to figure out what to do when a cryptocurrency has already fallen in value, you're already behind. You're squandering chances and will continue to do so because you don't have a strategy in place ahead of time.

It is critical to have a strategy in place. So, if bitcoin is now trading at $50,000 and you have $1,000 on hand to invest in the case of a

How to make more money during a crash

crypto price drop, you'll need to establish a strategy.

So, here's an example strategy:

If bitcoin is valued at $50,000, your strategy may be to purchase $100 worth if it reduces to $45,000, $200 worth if it lowers to $40,000, $400 worth if it drops to $35,000, and so on.

It doesn't matter so much what the actual statistics are, with the type of formula above; what counts is that you have a strategy.

Obviously, your portfolio may include more than simply bitcoin, so it will be a little more complicated than the example above, but you get the concept. This will save you from being paralyzed by indecision and either never purchasing at all or buying too early.

It also reduces impulsivity. And if you're thinking to yourself, "I can't do this; I'll be impulsive every time," there is something you can do. You may place a limit order for specified dip prices.

With that, you know there's actually an order out there — the price drops, the order fulfils automatically, and you don't have to do anything about it.

Now, if you don't feel comfortable leaving orders up and want to handle it yourself, CoinMarketCap lets you create alerts for when coins reach particular price points. You will get a notice or a ping when coins reach certain price points. You will purchase if the price is within your budget.

#2. Cryptocurrency shorting

This is a little riskier technique, but it is the second option to profit from a crypto meltdown.

This strategy is a little more tasking than the first one we mentioned. However, no one promised it would be simple.

It's useful to know how these things function.

Shorting cryptocurrency means betting against its price. If crypto falls in value, you profit, but if it rises, you lose money. It's the polar opposite of a typical crypto purchase.

However, this is highly risky, particularly in today's environment, when a single piece of news or a tweet from Elon Musk may cause the price of multiple cryptocurrencies to skyrocket.

How to make more money during a crash

This is particularly true for cryptocurrencies since good or bad news magnify or echoes across them, resulting in huge price movements.

In any case, if you're going to short crypto, you need to conduct some risk management beforehand to make sure you're okay with it.

How do you go about shorting bitcoin if you've chosen to do so? Many platforms trade crypto futures, but most of them are rather restricted in terms of what you may short or the numerous futures offers.

Binance, Deribit, BitMex, Kraken, and KuCoin are some of the more popular sites for crypto shorting. KuCoin is my favorite since it has certain unique features that make shorting more convenient. They sell normal coins that do technical futures trading in the background.

I will not go into much detail about crypto shorting since this is not a book on that. If you want to learn more about that, you may find a book that discusses that. Also, it is important to mention that it is highly risky. And I don't actively short crypto.

I'm more of a buy-and-hold investor. I don't do much shorting, but there are a million ways to earn money, and I want to give possibilities since someone who reads this could be interested in them. And, while we're on the subject of options, there are three other methods to earn money in a crash.

#3. Cryptocurrencies with price floors

This is similar to purchasing the dips, but I'll explain in greater detail. Bitcoin, for example, is volatile, but what is even more volatile? Altcoins.

Because altcoins are more volatile, they have the potential for deeper drops. This allows for a bigger upside as well as a modest reduction in risk in specific instances, which I shall explain.

When bitcoin falls in value, altcoins tend to fall even faster as individuals abandon projects. People who were day trading the currency swiftly abandon it, or the coin ceases to be a high confidence selection for them, and they abandon it.

Despite that, some individuals will still be holding on to that altcoin. These are people who are enthusiastic about the project. It's also possible that the currency has sunk so far into the abyss that people believe there's no use in selling now. There may also be others who intend to hodl indefinitely, regardless of what occurs. These are the people who will still have the currency.

You want such folks because they are the ones who are establishing a price floor. When you're down to only these folks, you're getting close to the price floor. And if you're jumping into one of the projects on the floor, this might really mitigate some of your risks.

The challenge now is: how do you determine the price floor? You can never be certain. You may get a sense of a price floor by following the cryptocurrency for a time and simply seeing where it goes or by looking at the chart and searching for price support levels.

Of course, this isn't an exact science, but it may serve as a starting point.

This means that even if the crypto market as a whole collapses, you could be able to buy a wonderful project at a low price with no risk.

Of course, there are exceptions; my personal rule of thumb is to only do it with projects that solve real-world issues and have financing. To put it another way, do it with projects that solve an issue while also generating a lot of money.

Algorand is a great illustration of this type of project; when crypto fell in May 2021, Algo fell with it and then sat at about 80 cents for months without moving. That 80 cents range became like the price floor.

This isn't to say that each cryptocurrency will perform similarly. However, it is better than buying at a high price and losing up to 40% the next day.

Cardano was one of the instances when I was able to do so directly. I believed it was a huge issue-solving project with a terrific team. There was no doubt that the price floor was about $1. So I bought as many red days as I could over the period of a few months. As a consequence, now that crypto has re-peaked, my investment has returned more than 150 percent.

Because I was confident in the project and understood how the market functioned, it felt like a turbo booster was strapped to my back. Of course, nothing is perfect, and I was ready to buy on days when the sky was red.

Let us now turn our attention to the fourth point.

#4. Lending as a liquidity source

One of the biggest disadvantages of buying the dip is that you may not always have extra cash on hand; you may have spent all you meant to invest, and the leftover funds are solely utilized for living expenses.

But, in my opinion, having money on hand is always important. I would still be up right now if I had gone all in on Cardano on the first day but at a 70 percent gain rather than a 150 percent gain. This is, without a doubt, a big difference.

There's a creative way to make money on the side with your coin while still having cash on hand. This involves lending USDT on KuCoin.

How to make more money during a crash

As previously said, we have a tendency to become a bit greedy with cryptocurrency, anticipating 60% annual returns on our money when a 10% or 20% return is excellent.

With USDT loans, you might potentially get those kinds of returns, or much more, depending on how crypto performs. You might get a return of up to 70% on your money if you invest wisely.

Here's how it works: you may borrow USDT from KuCoin for as little as seven days, and it'll normally be returned to you even sooner, in one, two, or three days.

So, if you keep just 20% of your crypto portfolio in USDT, ready to lend on the sidelines, and then deploy into a project if the price drops significantly, you'll almost likely make more money in the long term by picking those amazing projects.

If the value of bitcoin drops and you want to buy more, just stop your auto-loan and wait for your funds to be returned to you, after which you may invest them in bitcoin. You may take a little profit out of your USDT and resume the procedure when bitcoin achieves an all-time high.

I do it myself, as I already said, even though USDT is not my favorite currency. I normally lend a little more on the side just to have some income coming in.

#5: HODLING

The fifth and last approach to make money amid a crash is the simplest of them all: hodl.

Hold on for dear life. According to a wise man, you only lose money when you sell.

How to make more money during a crash

It isn't always the best advice, but it has shown to be true in several instances. There's no need to sell on a drop if you're confident in your assets, have done your homework, and have a long-term investment plan.

At least in the stock market, it has been established that individuals who purchase and hold virtually always outperform those who attempt to time the market. At least so far, the same can be said for the crypto market.

Hodling is by far the easiest and most successful way to end the year with more money than you now have.

SUMMARY

I hope you find these suggestions helpful.

Market crashes are an inescapable fact of life. And it's ideal if we're always prepared for such events.

You've learned about some of the factors that contribute to crashes, as well as how to prevent them. You've also seen the top five ways to multiply your money amid a slump in the market.

It's crucial to remember that you only lose money when you sell.

If you enjoyed reading this book, see what more the same author has to offer.

Also, don't forget to leave a review on Amazon for this book. It will help other crypto investors and enthusiasts like yourself decide whether or not to buy and read this book.

Printed in Great Britain
by Amazon